The Story of Our Lady of the Miraculous Medal

In a little country village in France, Fain-les-moutiers in Burgundy, there lived a hard-working farmer named Peter Labouré. He had a very devout wife and eleven active, happy children—eight boys and three girls. Zoé was the ninth of this group.

When Zoé was nine years old, her mother died. The girl took this very hard; she loved her mother very much. Mrs. Labouré had taught her children to love our Lady greatly. She tried to make them realize that the Mother of God was their heavenly Mother, also. This had impressed Zoé. When she lost her own dear mother, Zoé turned to our Lady with a deeper devotion, asking her to be truly her Mother. Her devotion deepened with the years.

Shortly after her mother's death, Zoé's Aunt Margaret, her father's sister, decided to take the two younger girls under her maternal care. So Zoé and her younger sister, Marie Antoinette, went to live with her. They stayed with their aunt for two years; then their father brought them home. He needed them to help him manage the house because his oldest daughter was planning to become a Sister of Charity.

Zoé was happy to be back home. She and Marie Antoinette set to work in the large farm house to make their father and brothers happy. Zoé kneaded the bread, did the washing, and carried the meals to the men working in the fields. Her joy was in caring for and feeding the 800 pigeons her father owned. The massive dove-cote still stands today.

When Zoé was twelve years old, she made her First Communion. It was from this time on that she desired to consecrate herself to God. Often on weekdays, early in the morning, she walked a mile and a half to the next village to assist at Mass either in the church or in the hospice which was under the care of the Sisters of Charity. Gradually the desire to serve God in the religious life began to take possession of her.

Being a dutiful daughter, Zoé waited with secret impatience until her younger sister would be old enough to take charge of the house. She began to undertake severe penances, fasting on Fridays and Saturdays, even when her work was heaviest. Throughout her well-filled day, she often had recourse to prayer.

Several times Zoé's hand was asked in marriage, but each time she refused. She wished for no other spouse but Jesus.

One night she had a dream which made a deep impression on her. She found herself in the village church. An old priest appeared and said Mass at which she devoutly assisted. At the end of Mass, he made a sign for her to approach, but she fearfully drew back. On leaving the church, she went to visit a sick person. She found the old priest there. He said to her: "My child, it is a good deed to visit the sick. You run away from me now, but one day you will be happy to come to me. God has His designs upon you. Do not forget it." Then she woke up. Zoé never forgot that dream and the old priest.

When Zoé was twenty-two years old, she felt that her sister was capable of replacing her. She asked her father for permission to become a sister. He emphatically forbade her to do so. He had given one daughter to the Church, and the thought that Zoé, his favorite, would leave him forever was something he could not bear. Zoé suffered in silence and begged God to take things in hand for her.

In order to distract her and perhaps to change her ideas, Zoé's father decided to send her away from the farm. He sent her to Paris with her brother Charles, who owned a restaurant. Zoé knew that God would not abandon her in a Paris restaurant. She stayed one year with Charles, bearing this hard trial as uncomplainingly as she could. She was miserable and out of place. When her sister-in-law, Mrs. Hubert Labouré, visited her in Paris, she noted this. She asked if she could bring Zoé to her home at Chatillon, where she conducted a boarding school. Here poor Zoé felt just as out of place, for the fashionable young ladies attending the Labouré school looked down on the uneducated peasant girl.

Mrs. Labouré was kind, tactful, and very farseeing. She wholeheartedly adopted Zoé's cause. She took Zoé to visit the Sisters of Charity in Chatillon. Zoé was astonished on entering the parlor to behold a picture, the perfect portrait of the old priest in her dream. When she asked who he was, she was told that he was the founder of the Sisters of Charity, St. Vincent de Paul. Her desire to become a Sister of Charity grew stronger than ever.

Mrs. Hubert Labouré finally persuaded Zoé's father to give his consent. She herself gave the money required as a dowry by the community, and she saw Zoé enter as a postulant at the house of the Sisters of Charity in Chatillon.

After a three months' test, Zoé left for Paris to begin her novitiate at the motherhouse at 140 Rue du Bac. She was given the name Sister Catherine. Her devotion and piety increased. She was humble, sincere and hardworking.

During the night of July 18, 1830, Sister Catherine was awakened by hearing her name called three times in succession. To her great surprise, she saw a beautiful child of about four or five years of age. He was dressed in white, and rays of light issued from his entire person. "Come," he said. "Come to the chapel; the Blessed Virgin is waiting for you."

Sister Catherine sat up in bed astonished but troubled. She slept in a large dormitory. The child reassured her: "Do not be afraid. It is half-past eleven and everyone is asleep. I will go with you."

Sister Catherine dressed quickly and followed her little guide, who kept always to the left side. The corridors were all brightly lighted, and, at the mere touch of the child's hand, the massive locked doors of the chapel opened. The chapel was brilliantly lighted. The candles on the altar, all burning brightly, reminded Sister Catherine of midnight Mass. She knelt at the altar rail and waited. Time seemed endless!

Towards midnight the child said, "The Blessed Virgin is coming. Here she is." Sister Catherine heard the rustling of silk as a beautiful lady walked into the sanctuary and seated herself in an armchair. Sister Catherine, following the impulse of her heart, threw herself at our Lady's feet, confidently resting her hands on Mary's knees. There she said she spent the sweetest moments of her life.

Mary instructed her as to how she was to act in moments of trial, and pointing to the altar, she told her that she should receive there all the consolations necessary for her. Our Lady predicted that terrible misfortunes were about to fall on France, that the throne would be overturned and the entire world would be afflicted by misery of some kind. There would be great danger then and forty years later, but the community would be protected by God and St. Vincent. Our Lady also told her that God had a special mission to confide to her. She would suffer many trials and contradictions, but she would be given grace so she was not to fear. After talking to Sister Catherine for a long time, our Lady withdrew and slowly disappeared. The child led Sister Catherine back to her dormitory, and, as she was getting back into bed, a distant clock struck two.

Shortly after this—in fact, in just a few days—the terrible Revolution of 1830 broke out. There was bloodshed and disaster for France. It did not last long, but it was terrible. Our Lady had predicted a worse disaster to take place in forty years. In 1870, the Franco-Prussian War caused much more trouble for France and for the Church.

Sister Catherine was instructed to tell no one about her visitor except her confessor. She told him everything except personal secrets confided to her by our Lady.

Our Lady had not told Sister Catherine what her special mission would be. She had come to prepare her for it. Sister Catherine found out what it was on November 27, 1830.

The sisters were all assembled in the chapel making their evening meditation. There was absolute silence. Sister Catherine heard the rustle of silk. Looking in the direction from which the sound came, she beheld our Lady. Mary was dressed in a shining white robe, a sky blue mantle and a white veil. She was standing on a globe, her feet crushing the serpent. In her hands she held a smaller globe which she seemed to offer to God. Suddenly her fingers were filled with jeweled rings, three on each finger. The brilliant rays that gleamed from the gems reflected on all sides.

As Sister Catherine was absorbed in what she saw, our Lady lowered her eyes on her and a voice said in the depths of her heart: "The globe that you see represents the entire world, especially France and each person in particular." Then the small globe disappeared and our Lady extended her radiant hands saying: "Behold the symbol of graces I shed upon those who ask me for them." Then Sister

Catherine understood how generous our Lady is to those who pray, how many graces she obtains for those who ask for them, and what a joy it is for our Lady to bestow them.

There now formed around the Blessed Virgin an oval shaped frame upon which appeared in letters of gold these words: "O Mary, conceived without sin, pray for us who have recourse to you!" Then Sister Catherine heard a voice: "Have a medal struck upon this model. All who wear it will receive great graces. Graces will be bestowed abundantly on those who have confidence." Suddenly the picture seemed to turn, and sister saw the reverse side. The letter M was surmounted by a cross with a bar at its base. Beneath the M were two hearts, one encircled by a crown of thorns and the other pierced with a sword. Twelve stars encircled this.

Sister Catherine was later asked what words were to be inscribed on the back of the medal. She asked our Lady who told her that the M with the cross, the two hearts, and the stars say enough.

Sister Catherine told Father Aladel, her confessor, about the apparition and the medal right away. This apparition appeared several times in the course of a few months, always in the chapel, either during Mass or during some of the religious exercises.

Months passed and the medal was not made. An interior voice soon reproached Sister Catherine. She knew that our Lady was not pleased. She told our Lady that Father Aladel did not believe her. Our Lady told her not to worry, that a day would come when he would do as she desired because he would fear to displease her.

When Father Aladel was told this, he knew that our Lady was not displeased with Sister Catherine but with him. He decided to act. Two years later, with the approval of the Archbishop of Paris, the medal of the Immaculate Conception was struck.

Medals were given out far and wide. So many cures and startling conversions resulted that people began to call the medal "miraculous." The archbishop ordered a canonical investigation made in reference to the origin and the effects of the medal because of the extraordinary and astonishing benefits derived from it. Today the medal is known and worn on every continent, and it still works marvels of grace through Mary's help. It is her gift to us reminding us of her presence and love.

The principal end of our Lady's apparitions to Sister Catherine was to develop devotion to the Immaculate Conception, and the medal was a means to this end. In 1830, through Sister Catherine, our Lady had sent

Father Aladel a special message. The Blessed Virgin wanted Father to found a confraternity of Children of Mary. Many blessings would be bestowed upon it. The month of Mary, May, would be celebrated with more solemnity. Father was puzzled about this. He knew that Sodalities of the Children of Mary already existed among the boys educated by the Jesuits, and that the Ladies of the Sacred Heart had formed similar associations among their pupils.

The more he pondered, the more he thought of our Lady's request, the more he realized that these sodalities were confined to a few isolated places and among a chosen class. Mary wanted this for the multitude of young boys and girls in the ordinary walks of life, surrounded by all the trials and dangers of the world. He was not too sure how to go about getting such a confraternity started. He used every opportunity he could to speak to the children and young people of our Lady's goodness and of the joy of belonging to her. God blessed his work. His listeners were affected by his words, and trial associations were formed in the orphanages and schools conducted by the Sisters of Charity.

Approval was obtained from the Holy Father to establish among the students attending the schools of the Sisters of Charity the pious confraternity under the title of the Immaculate Conception of the most Blessed Virgin with all the indulgences accorded to the Sodality of the Children of Mary established at Rome for the Jesuit students.

From this time, the Confraternity or Sodality of the Children of Mary spread rapidly in all quarters of the globe. A manual containing rules of the association, its privileges and obligations, was written by Father Aladel. The livery adopted by the Children of Mary was the miraculous medal suspended from a blue ribbon.

The sodalities had wonderful results. Piety and devotion increased in imitation of and love for our Lady. Parish priests the world over began to know of the sodality and its effects. They adopted it for their own people, young and old.

Since about 1930, the sodalities in the United States seem to have become more unified, more electrified. Many sodalities have become directly affiliated with the Jesuit sodality in Rome. Great Jesuits, like the late Father Daniel A. Lord, were very active in promoting greater love and devotion to our Lady by means of the parish sodalities, by "The Queen's Work," a sodality magazine, by pamphlets and books, and by the Annual Regional Sodality Conventions and Rallies held throughout the United States.

When Sister Catherine's novitiate training was completed, she was sent to an old folks' home, the House of Enghien, in Paris. There for forty-six years she helped to look after the old men and women who resided there. She was first placed in the kitchen. Amid the pots and pans she served God in serving His poor. She also had charge of the poultry yard. This must have reminded her of her childhood days back home on the farm. As the years passed, Sister Catherine, ever leading a life of humility and prayer, tenderly cared for and nursed the poor, distributing the Miraculous Medal to all whom she met.

No one knew that our Lady had appeared to her but Father Aladel, her confessor, and he was not allowed to reveal it to anyone. When he died, Sister Catherine was left with no one who knew her story.

A beautiful statue of Our Lady of the Miraculous Medal, with her hands extended as seen on the medal, had been placed over the main altar in the motherhouse chapel. Sister Catherine had told Father Aladel that our Lady also wanted one of her holding the globe. Father Aladel had made sketches and drawings but had died before having the statue made.

Sister Catherine was aging. She suffered from a painful rheumatism, and was no longer able to nurse and care for her poor. She acted as portress, welcoming visitors, mending the linens, and, above all, she prayed. She was worried about our Lady's statue.

One day Sister Catherine surprised her superior by bursting into tears. When her superior asked the cause, she told her she would tell her the next day if our Lady would give permission. The next day the superior was told the whole story of the apparitions concerning the medal and the statue. The superior promised her that the statue would be made according to the drawings. Sister Catherine was happy. She died peacefully within that year on December 31, 1876, knowing that our Lady of the globe would be in the motherhouse chapel.

Sister Catherine was canonized by Pope Pius XII on July 27, 1947. St. Catherine Labouré's body, perfectly preserved, rests under the altar of our Lady of the globe in the motherhouse chapel in Paris. Because the altar has a glass front panel, her body can be seen and venerated by all. There she reposes, dressed in the habit of the Sisters of Charity, awaiting the resurrection day.

The motherhouse chapel has been remodeled and made beautiful with a splendid mural of the first apparition and with lovely mosaics of pastel colors, bringing out the beauty of the white statues. Everything is conducive to prayer and recollection. The chair upon which our Lady sat is carefully preserved and regarded as a priceless treasure. It is close to the spot where St. Catherine lies.

The feast of our Lady of the Miraculous Medal is celebrated with great solemnity in the motherhouse chapel. On the very next day, St. Catherine Labouré's feast is celebrated there with great rejoicing.

Through a favored, humble daughter of St. Vincent de Paul, a Sister of Charity, our Lady made known her desire to bestow blessings and graces on those who ask for them. The medal is a symbol of Mary's love and a means for those who truly love Mary to show that love.

From *Cause of Our Joy*, by Sister Mary Francis Le Blanc, O. Carm. (St. Paul Editions, Boston).

Miraculous Medal Novena

Immaculate Mary

Immaculate Mary, your praises we sing;
You reign now with Christ, our Redeemer and King.

Chorus:
Ave, ave, ave, Maria!
Ave, ave, ave, Maria!

In heaven the blessed your glory proclaim;
On earth we, your children, invoke your fair name.

We pray you, O Mother, may God's will be done;
We pray for his glory; may his kingdom come.
Chorus.

We pray for our Mother, the Church upon earth;
And bless, holy Mary, the land of our birth.
Chorus.

Opening Prayer

In the name of the Father, and of the Son, and of the Holy Spirit. Amen.

Come, Holy Spirit, fill the hearts of your faithful and kindle in them the fire of your love.

Send forth your Spirit, and they shall be created. And you shall renew the face of the earth.

Let us pray. O God, you instructed the hearts of the faithful by the light of the Holy Spirit. Grant that by the same Spirit we may be truly wise and ever rejoice in his consolation, through Jesus Christ our Lord. Amen.

O Mary, conceived without sin, pray for us who have recourse to you. (Three times.)

Lord Jesus Christ, by countless miracles you have glorified the Blessed Virgin Mary, who was immaculate from the first moment of her conception. Grant that all who devoutly ask her protection on earth may eternally enjoy your presence in heaven. There with the Father and the Holy Spirit, you live and reign, God, forever and ever. Amen.

Lord Jesus Christ, for the accomplishment of your greatest works, you have chosen the weak things of the world, that no one may glory in your sight. For a better and more widespread belief in the Immaculate Conception of your Mother, you wanted the miraculous medal to be shown to St. Catherine Laboure. Grant that we may be filled with a humility like hers and glorify this mystery through our words and actions. Amen.

Memorare

Remember, O most gracious Virgin Mary, that never was it known, that anyone who fled to your protection, implored your help, or sought your intercession, was left unaided. Inspired with this confidence, I fly to you, O Virgin of virgins, my Mother. To you I come, before you I stand, sinful and sorrowful. O Mother of the Word Incarnate, despise not my petitions, but in your mercy hear and answer me. Amen.

Novena Prayer

Immaculate Virgin Mary, Mother of our Lord Jesus and our Mother, we are filled with the most lively confidence in your all-powerful and never-failing intercession, shown so often through the miraculous medal. As your loving and trustful children, we ask you to obtain for us the graces and favors we request during this novena, if these will be to our spiritual benefit.

Here, privately mention your petitions.

You know, O Mary, that we want our souls always to be the temples of the Holy Spirit, who hates sin. Obtain for us, then, a deep hatred of sin and that purity of heart which will attach us to God alone, so that our every thought, word and deed may be directed to his greater glory. Obtain for us a spirit of prayer and self-denial, that we may recover by penance what we have lost by sin and eventually enter that heavenly dwelling where you are the Queen of angels and of humanity. Amen.

An Act of Consecration to Our Lady of the Miraculous Medal

O Virgin Mother of God, Mary Immaculate, we dedicate and consecrate ourselves to you under the title of Our Lady of the Miraculous Medal. May this medal be for each one of us a sure sign of your affection for us and a constant reminder of our duties towards you. Ever while wearing it, may we be blessed by your loving protection and preserved in the grace of your Son. O most powerful Virgin, Mother of our Savior, keep us close to you every moment of our lives. Obtain for us, your children, the grace of a happy death, so that, in union with you, we may enjoy the happiness of heaven forever. Amen.

O Mary conceived without sin, pray for us who have recourse to you. (Three times.)

Closing Hymn

Mary, conceived without sin,
  Pray for us, pray for us;
Mary, conceived without sin,
  Pray for us who have recourse to you.

Our Lady of the Miraculous Medal

It is only an oval medallion
But 'tis a symbol of Mary's love.
She gave it for us to St. Catherine—
A source of blessings from above.
All graces come to us through Mary;
Jesus Himself wills it that way.
He tenderly loves His dear Mother
And will do what she chooses to say.
Mary's love for God is so perfect;
She wants our love for Him to be strong,
For love is proved by words and actions
And by courageously singing life's song,
The song of love, of praise, of valorous deeds
For God and for God alone
As we joyously trod the path of duty,
Lifting hearts besides our own.
Mary wants us to pray for our blessings,
To be grateful to God for all things,
And so she gives us a reminder—
A token—a medal—a medal with wings,
For faithfully to wear the medal
Is a symbol of love and of praise
And a silent prayer of intercession
Which to our heavenly Mother does raise.
Her hands are outstretched with blessings
For all of her children so true.
Call on her sincerely today;
She does have countless favors for you.

—Sister Mary Francis Le Blanc, O. Carm.

St. Paul Book & Media Centers

ALASKA
750 West 5th Ave., Anchorage, AK 99501 907-272-8183.

CALIFORNIA
3908 Sepulveda Blvd., Culver City, CA 90230 310-397-8676.
1570 Fifth Ave. (at Cedar Street), San Diego, CA 92101 619-232-1442
46 Geary Street, San Francisco, CA 94108 415-781-5180.

FLORIDA
145 S.W. 107th Ave., Miami, FL 33174 305-559-6715; 305-559-6716.

HAWAII
1143 Bishop Street, Honolulu, HI 96813 808-521-2731.

ILLINOIS
172 North Michigan Ave., Chicago, IL 60601 312-346-4228; 312-346-3240.

LOUISIANA
4403 Veterans Memorial Blvd., Metairie, LA 70006 504-887-7631; 504-887-0113.

MASSACHUSETTS
50 St. Paul's Ave., Jamaica Plain, Boston, MA 02130 617-522-8911.
Rte. 1, 885 Providence Hwy., Dedham, MA 02026 617-326-5385.

MISSOURI
9804 Watson Rd., St. Louis, MO 63126 314-965-3512; 314-965-3571.

NEW JERSEY
561 U.S. Route 1, Wick Plaza, Edison, NJ 08817 908-572-1200.

NEW YORK
150 East 52nd Street, New York, NY 10022 212-754-1110.
78 Fort Place, Staten Island, NY 10301 718-447-5071; 718-447-5086.

OHIO
2105 Ontario Street (at Prospect Ave.), Cleveland, OH 44115 216-621-9427.

PENNSYLVANIA
214 W. DeKalb Pike, King of Prussia, PA 19406 215-337-1882; 215-337-2077.

SOUTH CAROLINA
243 King Street, Charleston, SC 29401 803-577-0175.

TEXAS
114 Main Plaza, San Antonio, TX 78205 512-224-8101.

VIRGINIA
1025 King Street, Alexandria, VA 22314 703-549-3806.

CANADA
3022 Dufferin Street, Toronto, Ontario, Canada M6B 3T5 416-781-9131.

St. Paul Books & Media

50¢

ISBN 0-8198-5425-5